THOSE

Voices

THE DEMONS IN MOM'S MIND

TINA HARMON

DESIGNED BY:

GOLDMAN AGENCY
244 5th Ave h246, New York, NY
10001, United States

To two wonderful ladies. The first one is my mother, who has done the best that she knows how dealing with this sickness. The second lady is my grandmother, who no longer lives on this side of eternity. She loved my mom unconditionally, which made her life a little more bearable.

Momma, this illness is not your fault. Sometimes life deals a bad hand. You played your hand the only way you knew how. I believe that you understand your illness better and because of that understanding, you have given back to it as good as it has given you. I love you.

> "Mental illness leaves a huge legacy, not just
> for the person suffering it but for those around
> them"
>
> (Lysette Anthony).

PS to my son who is now plagued with the family curse and whom I love dearly. The following quote reminds me of you.

> "Sometimes it takes a wake-up call, doesn't it,
> to alert us to the fact that we're hurrying through
> our lives instead of actually living them; that we're
> living the fast life instead of the good life. And I
> think, for many people, that wake-up call takes the
> form of an illness"
>
> (Carl Honore).

Chapter 1

"Oh my god!" which is the only person other than the person themselves who understands the demons in a man's mind. I swear on a stack of Bibles that June 14, 1974, must have been the worst day of my life! It was a hot summer afternoon, and I had been out playing with my best friend. She had gone inside to get a drink, and I had to go to the bathroom really bad. I had played so long that I was walking cross-legged with my legs squeezing tight as a buffalo going down a manhole. I had grown to the ripe old age of seven, and there was nothing more exciting than playing with my best friend. This day would, however, be different. Something was wrong, terribly wrong. Where was Momma? As I was leaving the bathroom, she hadn't come to the door as she normally had to ask me if I was all right. It felt kind of strange that she wasn't concerned about me tearing too much toilet paper off the roll. That was her normal routine every time I went to the bathroom. She would peer in the door and scold me about my toilet paper use. As I flushed the toilet, I could hear what sounded like several different voices. I didn't see anyone come over, so I was anxious to finish my dirty doings so I could see who was out there.

I flushed the toilet, washed my hands, and dashed through the door with curiosity, but I was very much surprised. Nobody was there but Momma. I hadn't noticed her before, but she was there. Only it didn't look like her. She was standing in her bedroom in front of her mirror with a purple dress that displayed a huge protrusion. I knew she was going to have a baby, but what confused me was her hair. It looked like a lawnmower had busily hurried across it while missing spots, and that someone had tied multicolored ribbons on each piece of grass that was left behind. And to top it all off, she was talking to someone, but no one was there. "Do you hear them?" she asked. "Who, Momma? Who?"

"Those voices," she replied. "Those VOICES!"

I was a seven years old who was looking through the eyes of confusion. Seeing my mom standing in the mirror wearing a deep-purple dress with a belly the size of the biggest watermelon I could think of, with her haircut and different color ribbons tied to each little ponytail, talking to made-up people was frightening. That was a sight that would haunt me the rest of my life, and the words *those voices* would ring through eternity.

You see, this thing called life started out all wrong. I was born on September 30, 1966, to a sixteen-year-old mother, who was manipulated and hoodwinked with a whole lot of lies and promises from this young gangster in the neighborhood. He, my father, was very cunning and probably even cute, and he had a way with girls. At least one girl that I know. There I was bursting on the scene, making my grandmother the youngest "granny" in town. In those days, when you had a baby, there was a lot of pressure on you to get married. The real pressure was to already have been married before you have kids. Neither one of those plans worked with my parents. Because by the time I was three months old, my father was shipped off to prison, and that left my mother single with child.

My granny just wasn't going to put up with that nonsense, so she and her best friend decided to do some matchmaking. That's when the evil plan began. My granny was never one to mince words, so I was told that the conversation went a little like this: "Red, you need to meet Martha's nephew. His name is John, and he seems to like you."

"I'm not interested in meeting anyone," she replied.

"You really should."

"Who do you think wants a girl who has a baby these days?"

"I suggest you meet him, young lady, and not miss your chance of having a husband." This young man has a job and everything to offer."

Ms. Martha had this young handsome nephew who she thought would be perfect for my mom, so the introductions began. You talking about a shotgun wedding. They met, went on a few dates, and were coerced and pushed so hard to get married, and they did. Because before I reached the ripe old age of one, they were married.

How do you get to know someone that fast? My granny didn't care. All she knew was that her daughter was married, and now it was okay to have babies. This was the beginning of a nightmare.

John worked for a prominent business and was making good money. We moved into a small apartment in downtown Cincinnati that was rat infested, cold, and dark. My earliest memory was when I was two, my mom had given birth to my brother. So now there were two children in the house. I remember sitting in the dark with candles burning. It was really cold, and I was hungry. "I'm hungry," I said as we made our way with one candle to the kitchen table.

"It'll be all right," Mom said as she grabbed my hand, holding tight to my baby brother. She started what seemed to be some sort of chanting. She was doing something I didn't understand. I was familiar with the chanting because I had seen her perform that ritual before, but I had no idea what she was doing, so I was waiting in anticipation for a meal. It seemed as though every time she chanted, someone would knock on the door; and instantly, a plate of food would somehow magically appear that we shared. I came to find out later that my mom was not chanting. She was praying, and every time she prayed, someone would show up to the door with food for us to eat.

John was never home and didn't buy food, neither did he pay the gas and electric bill, and my mom was always worried, but she never said anything to granny about it. In those days, you kept whatever business you had to yourself. It was already bad enough that she had two children and was struggling to keep us safe and fed. She didn't need criticism from others.

After being married a little over a year, Mom was finally realizing something about her new husband. He had a gambling problem. The gambling was so serious that it sent our family spiraling into torment and uncertainty. It was something that his whole family did.

They had all-night card games, went to bingo, and John took it a step further. He shot dice on street corners. He was the type of man who gambled his whole paycheck. He had no sense of responsibility. He didn't care that he had a wife and two children. He did what he loved best, gambling, while my mom was left borrowing from neighbors and constantly praying to God for help.

Thank God for the little old lady who lived on the corner from us. She helped my mom a lot. She did my hair in her parlor, and she would send plates of food home with us. "Here, Red, take this with you. I know it's not much, but it just might hold you for a couple days." She was the sweetest thing, and she and my mom became good friends. There was also a man who lived next door to us. He must have been concerned, and he gave us food from time to time. All these things took place, yet Mom never said a word to Granny. She knew that she had messed up by having me so young, and she wasn't prepared to be criticized about a failed marriage. Furthermore, she was told to stay with her husband no matter what. That was the rule, and you just didn't break it.

Chapter 2

Life seemed to move very slowly. The days of being hungry increased, and there appeared to be no end to the madness. One day, John came home really excited. He apologized to Mom and explained to her that he was buying her a new house. "I found the perfect house, and things are going to be great. I promise." This was his way of making things up to her. We were moving to a new town, moving out of the *ghetto* of downtown where the church bells rang, the cars passed, people fought and cursed, and children wrote distasteful things on buildings and sidewalks. We were moving to a top-of-the-line neighborhood into this beautiful two-bedroom brick house with a huge backyard for playing. It was quiet and calm, and life seemed as though it would be better. I had a room that I shared with my brother, but it was nice. As I stood outside on the front porch, the wind whistled though the silence, and all was well.

I started preschool at Corinthians Baptists Church, and Mom walked me to school over the railroad tracks that were located at the end of our street four days a week. It was a new experience. We had a new house, we had food, and Mom was happy. For the first time in her marriage, things looked promising. The lights were on, and that damp musty smell was gone. The alleys were gone. The darkness was gone. The empty stomach was gone.

I jumped over the rainbow from preschool and enjoyed the summer with my little brother. We played records that had books to them. We learned how to read, and we made new friends. My favorite story was *Peter and the Wolf.* I loved to listen to that amazing music as the story was told about a boy meeting a wolf and outsmarting him. During those moments, there was not a care in the world. We were being kids. We were eating good food. I had my own bed, and all summer we played and played and played.

Summer went by, and it was time for me to go to kindergarten at the big school, Kennedy Elementary. I remember crying all day. "I don't want to stay." "Where's my momma?" I sobbed and sobbed. Although I had already attended preschool, things seemed extremely scary in that big new building. After three or four days, I calmed down and began to enjoy walking to school with my mom and brother. Then I met my first friend. She had moved next door with the neighbors. Her mom had been killed, and the Moores had adopted her so she could have a secure place to be. We played with each other every day. We played dolls, jump rope, jacks, and we sometimes played house incorporating my little brother to be the baby. That year, I had the time of my life. I had a new best friend. I went to a cool new school, and my mom sent us to camp where we learned how to swim and ride horses. We were able to go swimming at Kennedy School almost every day, and things appeared to be going just fine.

Unfortunately, things did not last. Underneath all that bliss, darkness was setting in. It was creeping in like a sidewinder on a hot day in tall weedy grass. Not only was it creeping in, it would soon cover us like the canopy of trees found in the jungles of Africa, not allowing any light to come through. It would later devour us like a Tyrannosaurus Rex eating its young.

I finished kindergarten and went on to first grade when the darkness began taking hold of our lives again. You see, it never really left us. We were on borrowed time, and time had run out. As the minutes rushed by, I began to recognize remnants of the past. Yeah, it was subtle, but at the end, it was like a flood. Food started getting scarce. John was never at home. The darkness was upon us, and the shadows overtook us, and we began spiraling through a dark hole of no return.

At the end of first grade, John went into Romans Psychiatric Hospital, and we were told that he had a nervous breakdown. Mom was pregnant, and I remember thinking to myself, *What's a nervous breakdown? How do you get one? Is it catchy? Maybe Mom would catch it, then me, then my brother.* I remember feeling scared and anxious. My body was shaking as if someone had jumped from behind the bushes and startled me. I needed some answers, but no one would talk about it. Mom didn't say much other than he would be all right, and that he would have to stay in the hospital for a little while. "How long is a little while?" I asked.

"I don't really know, but soon," she replied. "You just go outside and play. I'll handle this."

So, of course, I went on playing and laughing as usual. I didn't have any idea that having a nervous breakdown meant that you were crazy as we kids would put it. As time passed, I found out that John was crazy. His mind had shut down on him, and he was no longer able to cope with the stress of life. I wasn't sure what the stress was, but I would soon find out.

It was the summer of 1974 when John came home. Mom was pregnant and due to deliver the baby in a couple of months. About two weeks after he was home from the hospital, John started right back with the gambling routine. It seemed as though gambling was the stress factor that had driven him crazy. John gambled his whole paycheck, and the days of being left in the dark and hungry returned. He would also stay gone all weekend while my mother cried her eyes out yet remained silent about that harsh and bitter reality of having married a sick, sick man. Yes, I say sick because gambling is a disease. It's one that eats through a family like cancer to the bone. It infests your very being, and it clouds your judgment and ability to reason between right and wrong. It leaves families hopeless and distraught to the bitter end.

Chapter 3

Momma had one of the prettiest flower gardens in the whole neighborhood. That year, the flowers hadn't grown. My brother and I were able to dig in the garden and make mud pies, throw dirt, and get super muddy. I threw dirt at him, he threw dirt at me, and before you know it, dirt was everywhere. "Stop," I yelled. "You got dirt in my hair." My brother just kept throwing dirt. My mother appeared out of nowhere and startled us.

"Quit throwing that dirt and move over, I'm getting ready to plant my flowers." Mom had gone to the store to buy flowers since hers hadn't bloomed. "I don't know why these flowers haven't grown," she said. She was big and pregnant, barely able to bend over, but she was determined to have her pretty flower garden. As she was digging, the oddest thing happened. She dug up this ugly doll. It had pins and needles sticking in it, and it appeared to be very old. That night, Mom made a fire and began to burn the doll. Smoked filled the air, and dogs started barking out of nowhere. It was as though the world was spinning out of control, and quite frankly, I don't know where the barking came from seeing we only had one little dog in the whole neighborhood. Maybe I heard them because Momma heard them. After that night, Mother was never the same. Things started getting pretty weird as each day passed. There were no flowers in the garden because she never got a chance to plant them after digging up that doll. Mom was saying and doing strange things, and although I noticed these sudden but quick changes, I kept playing and being a kid the way I always did.

A couple of nights later, she had my brother and I out late walk-ing up and down our little dead-end street, looking for my father. We were asking the neighbors who were sitting on their porches that night if they had seen our father. "Go ask Mr. Smith if he has seen your father."

"Excuse me, Mr. Smith, have you seen my dad?"

"No, sweetheart, but I'm sure he'll be home soon."

I knew right away that something was seriously wrong with my mother, but what? I didn't know. We walked up the street, down the street, and my mom had this estranged look on her face. It was as if she was in another world. She was looking around, but what was she seeing? She didn't say anything else the whole time we walked. She just looked. We finally returned home, and we all got in her bed and fell asleep. Sometime during the night, my father came home and put us in our own bed.

The next day, I was outside playing with Jan and had to use the bathroom. I remember going into the house to use the bathroom. I was in a hurry. I waited too long and was about to pee my panties. I heard Mom talking, and I was wondering who she was talking to. As I approached the door of her room, I saw a sight that would haunt me for the rest of my life. My mother was standing in the mirror talking to no one I could see and cutting all of her hair off. She had different color ribbons tied to little pieces of her hair that she hadn't yet cut, and she looked as though she was possessed. "Momma, what's wrong?" I asked with a scared and puzzled look on my face.

"Do you hear them?" she replied.

"Hear who?"

"Those voices coming from the attic."

"Momma, you're scaring me. I don't hear anything."

"Those voices," she cried, "they're trying to get me, but I hear them."

I ran outside to get my little brother and went to the neigh-bor's house to inform her that there was something wrong with my mother. "Mrs. Moore, there's something wrong with my mother, and I don't know what to do."

"Okay, sweetheart, go home and lock the door. I will call your grandmother."

I took my little brother in the house and locked the door and waited. Mom was still walking around and talking to what seemed to be invisible people. Suddenly, out of nowhere, the phone rang, and it was my grandmother. "Let me speak to Red" she said.

"Momma, it's Granny. She's on the phone for you."

Mom looked at me as if she didn't know who I was, and then she wrote on a piece of paper these words: "Tell your grandmother that I'm an ear, and I can't come to the phone and talk to her, because ears can only listen, not talk." I read the paper to Grandmother, and that night, she came to get us.

In a twinkling of an eye, our lives changed. Mother was put into an insane asylum, and we went to live with Granny. My father had to be put back in a psychiatric clinic. Somewhere in the midst of all that chaos, Mom gave birth to my baby brother. Things for me became a blur. My next memory was that of having a baby brother. Me, him, and my other brother all had sores in our head that had a bad odor, and my baby brother had them the worst. The smell was that of rotting flesh, and all of our hair fell out. No one in the family knew what to do about it. My granny finally sought medical attention, and the sores began to heal. This was the most difficult time of my life. This was the time that my childhood stopped. Granny took us in, but she worked. There was this new little creature called a baby, and someone had to care for it. What does a seven-year-old know about taking care of a baby? What does a seven-year-old know at all? That summer went by rather slowly. I had lost my best friend, and I had to stay in the house and clean, cook, and take care of my little brothers. It seemed as though it was me against the world. What does a seven-year-old know about the world? Not much.

Chapter 4

When the summer was over, I started school at Parham Elementary. I was the new kid on the block, and nobody liked me. The kids teased me every day, and it seemed like it would never end. Home wasn't much better. Every day, I was burdened down with chores and responsibilities. I didn't know where my mother was, and no one was talking about her or her condition. I was wondering if she had died or would I ever see her again. I was confused. I was so lonely. I was afraid. I was little. I didn't know what to tell my brother when he would look up at me and say, "Where's Mama? Terry, where is Mama?" I didn't know what to tell him, so I would make up stuff like: "she went to the store, and she'll be shopping for a while," or "she's on vacation." I just didn't know what to say. As time went by, I started having headaches every day around the same time. I went to my grandmother, and she took me to the doctor, and he couldn't find anything wrong. I finally asked my grandmother where my mother was, and she replied, "Your mother is sick and could be in the hospital for a very long time"

"Can I go see her?" I replied.

"Soon, you will see her."

Later that evening, I sat my little brother down and told him our mother was sick. I didn't know what kind of sickness she had. That would come later. He began to cry. "I don't want her to be sick. When is she getting out of the hospital?"

"I don't know. Soon, I hope."

Later finally came when we were to go visit mother. I remember going to the hospital and sitting in this room. My grandmother was talking to this lady behind a big glass window. All of a sudden, I heard this buzzing sound, and my grandmother took my hand, and we walked through this big metal door that opened on its own. We walked to this huge room that had tables, chairs, some games, and a TV. There were people in the room smoking cigarettes and playing cards. A few minutes later, my mom came in the room. She came and sat next to me and didn't say anything. She had a look on her face as if she didn't know who I was.

"Hi, Mama, how are you?" I said slowly and frightened, unsure of what to say.

"Hi," she said with no emotions or facial expressions. Most of the visit was silent. As I began to look around, there were people talking to themselves and screaming at the nurses, and I heard someone say that the nurses were trying to poison them. At that very moment, I knew my mother was mentally ill. I began to understand what my grandmother meant by sick. This was a different kind of sickness. This was a life-altering sickness, a sickness that had no cure. Mother eventually said a few words that made no sense to me, and I knew from her tone of voice that she was not herself. My world as I knew it would no longer be the same. Thoughts began running through my mind: No one must know about this. People would be cruel and would possibly say things like, "your mother is crazy," and this sent me into a frenzy. At all cost, my friends must not know. I would be the talk of the school. The kids would laugh at me. All those thoughts were ringing in my head. What was I going to do about this? It was then that I began to understand that my mother was crazy, which was the term used in those days, but what she really was, manifested itself in the form of a doctor's diagnosis of paranoid schizophrenia. Mother stayed in the hospital for about a year, it seemed, then she came to live with us at Granny's house.

I thought that I was living in a nightmare before with the gambling and the hunger. That was nothing compared to what would happen in days, months, and years to come.

In the meantime, my father had come to live with us after they released him from the hospital, and he wasn't himself either. These two wonderful people whom I called mom and dad were complete strangers to me. What happened to them? Who did this? Are they ever going to be them again? Time would tell it all.

Mother came home and got settled in. She stayed in her room for the first three days. When she finally surfaced, I brought her the baby, and she rejected him. "Who is this little man? I don't know him, get him away from me." The baby started crying because he was afraid of her. "The little men are out to get me, can't you see them? Don't you hear them?" she said. I took my little brother into the living room to watch TV. A few minutes later, Mother was walking through the house looking up at the ceiling, saying things like, "I hear you, you can't have my soul. Listen. Can you hear them? They are on top of the roof. They are telling me to come outside, and God doesn't love me. Make them stop!" she screamed.

My grandmother heard her scream and came downstairs. "What's the matter, Red? What happened?" She stopped talking and resumed that blank stare that consumed a great part of her. "Come on, Red, let's sit down. Tell me what happened."

Again, complete silence fell in the room as Mother said nothing. She began walking slowly toward the stairs. One by one, she went up and vanished into her room.

The baby was crying, and my mind was wondering, *What just happened? Why was she talking that way?* You see, I really did not understand the fullness of having schizophrenia, nor did I understand the torment of a person's mind.

A couple of days later, Mother was in her room crawling around on the floor and making animal noises. My grandmother went into the room and tried to get her up. "Come on, Red, it's time to take your bath and put on your clothes"

"Let me go! You're trying to poison me," she said loudly with authority. "I'm not putting on any clothes. There is something in those clothes. I know, they told me."

My grandmother exited the room shaking her head in despair. "Terry, why don't you go and try to help your mom put on some clothes. Maybe she will listen to you."

There I stood on the threshold of the door to her room scared out of my wits, but willing to try and help any way that I could.

After all, she was my mother. I entered the room with caution, and I approached my mother who was still crawling around naked chanting, something that was strange in nature. "Mama, come on. Let's put on your clothes." My main focus was to get her dressed so that my brothers wouldn't see her that way. She got up from the floor to my amazement and put on her clothes. This was day one of a lifetime of terror.

About a month went by and getting Mother dressed became a ritual of some sort. There was always Granny starting out, trying to get her dressed, but everything would end up with me ultimately getting her to put on her clothes. She hadn't bathed, and that was becoming a big problem. My baby brother would look at her through the door at times, and she would reply, "Get that little man away from door. Who is he? What does he want?" On occasion, he would cry as if he knew she was his mother and didn't want anything to do with him. Things were an utter mess. Mother had to go back to the hospital for a while, and another lapse in time was created in our lives. Again, another year went by. Summer came. I made a few friends, and life was sort of normalizing.

Chapter 5

My grandmother was working every day, and I was coming home doing my usual duties that no eight-year-old should have had to do. Mother was safe within the compounds of the asylum, and life was moving on, or so we thought.

Early one morning, Granny got a call. "Mrs. Brown, your daughter Red has escaped from the institution. The nurse went in to administer her medication, and she was gone. We have looked everywhere. We want to extend our apology and let you know that we are doing everything we can to find her. If she shows up at your house, we would appreciate it if you would call us immediately."

A panic went through the house like wildfire. "John, Red has escaped from the hospital. They called just now and they have looked everywhere for her. Can you take me around to places you think she may have gone?" My father, who had not long been released from the hospital, got his car keys, and he and Granny went looking for her. No one informed me that this was taking place. I just overheard it like everything else I knew I just heard it. My father and Granny looked for her for about three to four hours and returned home empty-handed. The police had already been notified, so looking for Mother became a waiting game. It seemed like days before we would find her. Then she finally showed up at my uncle's house and was returned to the hospital. She never told us where she was for three days. She just appeared as quickly as she disappeared. I didn't care where she was. I was just glad that they had found her.

I remember feeling really sad and lonely. I had no one to talk to. I was the oldest, and both of my little brothers depended on me.

I couldn't tell them everything that was happening. They were too young. It's a bad thing when you have no one to turn to. I lived in a house with my grandparents and my uncle, who was practically grown and had a life of his own. Who was I to turn to? Who was I to lean on? All these things happening, how much could I take? I prayed every day, and I would imagine that I was someplace else, that I was someone else.

"Why was God doing this to me?" I would ask, "and why did he do this now?" I was a child who should have been outside playing in the yard, making friends, or hanging out with all the other kids, yet I was in darkness hiding from the rest of society so no one would know about Mother. God forbid a friend would see her in her condition. I would be the laughing stock of every crazy joke, every evil prank, and every poking moment would be directed at me. When I went to school, I didn't talk to anyone. I was afraid they would know as if they could read my thoughts. I didn't want a friend. I was afraid that they would ridicule Mother and tell my secret. Kids are evil, and they have ways of making you feel bad about yourself. On top of that, the neighbor kids would chase my brother and I home from school every day. There were five of them, and we had come to fear them like nobody's business. My life was a total mess, so I was always imagining myself someplace else. I would close my eyes tight and squeeze them as if I would never open them again. Then I would think about a place, anyplace that had flowers, where the wind was blowing hard and wild, and I would imagine myself being blown around, picked up, and tossed to and fro. This was how I dealt with my horrible surroundings, my reality, and my life.

I visited my mom in the hospital as often as possible. She would come home as often as she could. Many times she was home for a short period of time, always having to be taken back by force. She wouldn't take her medicine for some made-up reason or another, and the police would be called. It would take several police officers and a set of handcuffs to get her in the police car. She had the strength of Hercules and the might of Thor. She was stronger than any person I knew. I saw her holding on to the back of a couch and having to have two or three men get her off. Those days were like bloody

Sundays. The neighbors would be gawking, and people came from other streets to see why police lights were flashing at our house. Our address became famous. The police practically knew why they were called, and they knew my mother by name. I started to wonder if my mother would ever get better. Questions came to my mind about her being this way forever. Would she ever lead a normal life? Was she ever going to be my mom again? Questions at the time that seemed as though would never be answered.

Time went on with Mother not really getting much better. She finally started showing improvements, and by this time, a couple of forgotten birthdays had passed, and I had reached the ripe old age of ten. They had given her several different medical cocktails and had found the mixture that would stabilize her. She came home, and she was home for at least a year before any other episodes would happen. She got herself a boyfriend, and I thought finally she was all right. She introduced me to my biological dad, and things were going great. I had three new little brothers and a stepmother that was wonderful and easy to talk to. I finally had an outlet to the madness in my life. I had an escape place. Mother got a divorce from my stepdad John and moved forward with what appeared to be a normal life.

Chapter 6

Two years had gone by, and I reached the age of twelve. I was old enough to stay up all night on weekends, and most of the time, I did watching old scary movies. Mother was taking her medicine, and she was back to the mother I had remembered.

One night, my aunt and I was hanging out. We recorded music on her reel-to-reel recorder, and we ended up watching scary movies with my favorite fright night man Cool Ghoul. My mother was up for a while, walking around the house as she normally did. Sort of watching me off and on. My aunt had retired for the night, and I was determined to see the sunrise. It had gotten rather late, but I stayed up watching a Vincent Price movie. Mom poked her head in the dining room. "You ain't sleepy yet?" she said.

"No, ma'am."

"Don't you think you should be going to bed now?"

"I'm all right. I want to finish this movie." I convinced her that I was fine, and she left me alone. I kept hearing her walking around upstairs, but I was consumed with my movie and didn't think anything of it.

As the movie progressed, I heard a knock on the door, and I felt like I had jumped to the moon and back. I remembered thinking, *Who could that be at this hour?* I had aunts who always hung out late and often dropped by unannounced. Maybe it's one of them. I went to the door and pulled the curtain back and didn't see anyone. The first thing I thought was that the neighbor kids were playing a joke and had come knocking on the door and ran. I stood at the door and peeped through the curtain where no one could see me, hoping to catch those kids. As I was looking out, another knock came to the door, but I didn't see anyone. How could someone be knocking at the door, and I don't see them. After all, I was looking out through a slit in the curtains. Was I imagining it? It was those scary movies I was looking at. They had somehow become a reality. I was becoming frightened by every knock. The knocking was getting persistent, so I thought the kids were knocking at the bottom of the stairs off to the side where I couldn't get a visual. Yeah, that's it, they're on the side of the steps. So I flung the door open, and much to my surprise, there, lying at the top of the stairs, was my mother. The moment was silent. Chills went up and down my spine. The blood rushed to the top of my head, and I felt faint.

"Oh my god," I screamed. "What happened, Momma? Who did this to you? How did you get outside?"

Her words to me would haunt me to this day. "I jumped out of the third-floor window. Call an ambulance."

I ran upstairs screaming to my grandmother who thought I was having some bad dream. "Granny, Granny, Momma, she . . . she . . . come quickly, hurry up."

"Calm down. I can't understand you."

I literally pulled her downstairs to see for herself. At that moment, things went black for me. I was standing there, crying and watching my mom lay on that floor, and there was nothing I could do about it. My mind went blank. I don't remember the ambulance, the police, or any of that. I remembered hearing sirens, but I didn't see anything. More darkness, gross darkness. It was surrounding me, covering me, consuming me, and overshadowing me. I couldn't breathe. I was numb. I couldn't move. What would I tell my brothers now? My aunt ran downstairs, and I sort of came back.

"Are you okay? What happened?"

I attempted to explain to her, but my mouth wouldn't move. My grandmother had gotten her purse and needed a ride to the hospital. She started telling my aunt what happened, and she couldn't believe something like that had happened. That night would haunt everyone involved. Talking about a scary movie. That night, I lived one. It was the scariest movie of all. It was my life. It was so traumatizing that it changed my sleeping patterns. I once slept like a dead person. Now I hear everything that moves, and I suffer with sleep loss.

Mother was in the hospital with a broken back and a few cracked ribs. She had attempted, for the first time in her life, suicide. What was she thinking? Why would she want to leave us? We needed her. No matter how sick she was, she was still our mother, and kids need their mother.

My brother asked me the next day where our mother was, and I had to be the one to tell him that she was in the hospital. I made him believe that she was in there for her usual stay. He had gotten used to her goings and comings. I couldn't bring myself to tell him that our mother had attempted suicide. I just couldn't tell him. Sometimes when you look at the face of a loved one and they have a look of innocence, you just can't bring yourself to destroy that.

Mother stayed in the hospital for about six weeks, and when she came home, she had a body cast, but she could walk. Once Mother came home from the hospital, I was curious about why she had attempted such a drastic feat. When I talked to her about it, she told me it was the voices she heard. She said that the voices had told her to jump so that she could end her misery and be with Jesus. When she fought the urge to jump, she said that the voices commanded her to jump and told her that this would be the best thing that ever happened to her. At the time, the voices were strong, and they over-powered her natural thinking process. Her mind created a staircase flowing from the third-floor window down into the backyard. She was convinced that she was going to be with Jesus, and she walked out of that window in a delusional state that almost ended her life. Although she was on her medication, she was still exhibiting some symptoms. She couldn't get rid of those voices. They rode her like a farmer riding his tractor day and night to get the job done. The voices had a mission. They wanted to destroy the person within, my mother.

Granny stayed home from work for about three weeks to care for her, then everything else was left up to me as usual. Plus I still had two little ones to look after. Every day after school, Granny left for work, and I stayed home to tend to the house. Mother had to be watched almost around the clock, and so did the baby. I had little or no time to spend with the two friends that I had or myself. This was a never-ending saga. It seemed like months and months before I could escape to my dad's house. The visits with him began to be less because I just didn't have the time.

Granny eventually stopped working, but when she wasn't working, she was out of town with her church group or taking Mother out of town to see some psychic or soothsayer. She really was trying all she knew to help Mother to get well. She went to one guy who told her that someone had done something to Mother really evil, like some spell or something. She went to another place that had her bathing Mother in some weird herbs. None of these things worked, and I think she paid money for them. Life for me picked up a little. I got to go out and play more and hang out with my friends. I met more friends and got caught up in the world and all that it had to offer. I fell into using marijuana and drinking wine so that I could cope with having a dysfunctional family life. I did most of it to help me deal with going home. I found myself more and more relaxed and mellowed out. This became my new way of dealing with my mom. Overtime I was able to hang out with my dad more and having just a little bit more fun with my other family.

Although I would be miles away at my dad's, Mother was always in the back of my mind. My heart was always with her. She was still wearing her cast, and crazy talk was still coming out of her mouth. She always thought that my granny was out to get her. She thought people were talking about her all the time. She was paranoid all the time. This too was part of her disease. It came with voices, and those voices made her scared. The voices planted things in her head, and she believed them to be true. She didn't trust anyone especially Granny. Surely her own mom was out to kill her. At least in her mind.

Chapter 7

About three months passed and Mother was still wearing her cast and all was calm. "Have you seen your mother?"

"Yes, ma'am, she went into the basement. I think she is washing some clothes. I hadn't really noticed how long she had been down there. I just remembered seeing her go through the door."

Granny went in the basement and found her unconscious on the floor. "Terry, call the police. We need an ambulance. Something is wrong with your mom."

I rushed to the phone and dialed the police. "Hello, my name is Terry, and I live at 3048 Cline Street. Something is wrong with my mom, and we need an ambulance."

"Right away, ma'am."

They knew this address. They had been here many times before. The ambulance came quick. They informed my grandmother that Mother would be all right. Mother had decided to go into the basement where she took a whole bottle of sleeping pills. Again there was another episode at our house. Ambulance, police, and the whole nine yards, again another scene. What was I to do now? I thought that stuff was over. Didn't she learn anything from all the other times? Was she doing this on purpose? My mind was racing as I'm sure hers was too after hearing voices telling her to, "end it, finish what you started, you're really worthless now." Audible voices that instructed her to get the pills and finish the job. Voices that were too strong for her to resist. But as a child, you have no sense of things like people hearing voices. You never understand voices. What voices? I didn't hear them. What was she talking about all the time? "Those voices."

Was she making things up? Somebody, tell me please. Help me to understand. But there was no one. All you know and think is that something has to be done, but what? By whom? My granny didn't understand. How was she to tell me? My aunts and uncle were afraid of my mom. They wouldn't dare come near. My stepdad was out of the picture. I think he sort of knew what was happening since he had had a nervous breakdown too. All I wanted to know was who had the answers? Who were the voices? Would they ever stop talking? Somebody, please. Somebody, please help me. It was ringing in my spirit and in my heart.

Mother came home after three days in the hospital and resumed living with her cast. I'm not sure how long she was supposed to keep the cast on, because two or three days after she returned home, she went to the basement again. This time she climbed into the washtub, lay in there, and soaked her cast until it was soft enough to cut off. Again, Granny found her downstairs and had to call the ambulance to take her to the hospital. This time she stayed for about a week. Again I was left to tend to the house and explain things to my brothers. This time I told the whole truth, and my brother and I cried together.

"Sit down, boo, I have something to tell you. Our mother is mentally ill, and that means crazy. She has tried a few times to kill herself. She says that she hears voices in her head, and I don't know if she will ever get better."

"Is that why she keeps going to the hospital?" he asked.

"Yes."

He started crying. I started crying, and there we were crying with the little one looking puzzled. He was much too young to understand. My brother and I cried for a while, and he never was the same little boy again. I don't know what happened to him, but he was totally different. His behavior at school changed. He was in trouble a lot. He started being put in boys' town, and he just has not been the same. I often wondered if I should have told him or should I have waited another year. I just couldn't keep it any longer. I had to get it out of my system before I too start hearing voices.

Chapter 8

When Mother came home, she was fine. For the first time in a long time, she was quite normal. She had a hump on her back, but she was walking. She was on a different medicine, which seemed to have stabilized her more. She got a new boyfriend. She moved into her own apartment, and she lived fairly well. Her boyfriend became her rock. He knew her condition, and he made sure that she took her medicine every day. She was with him for about seventeen years. I think it was he that helped keep her on track. He took good care of her. The voices stopped, and she lived normal for ten years. By that time, I had went on with my life. After graduation, I signed up and went into the Army where I met my husband. I had left to escape all of the pain of my youth.

About a year after I left, Mother relapsed, and I had to go home and help my grandmother get her into the hospital. She started thinking her boyfriend was doing things to her, and she held up a knife at the neighbors thinking that they were plotting against her. Things were off track. Somehow she had missed too many days of not taking her medicine. Her boyfriend didn't live with her. He was married. He had done the best he could seeing after her, but he too had failed this time. She had started that spiral all over again. The voices came back, and every time they told her something, she believed them. They were as real to her as this book you're reading.

Every time the voices talked to Mother, she would hear them and remember what they said at a later time, but she could not control them. She could always recall what they said, but she couldn't shut them up or stop them. She said it was as if someone was talking to her. Then possessing her body and doing what the voices said. For the first time in my life, I understood what she was saying. I had grown up now and was a lot more mature and understanding. I knew at that very moment that she hadn't made them up. She was really hearing someone talking in her head. I realized how frightening that must be. It must sound like God. Illuminated voices out of thin air. I can only imagine how terrified she must feel when that happens.

Although I had left Cincinnati and my mom, the problem was still there. I couldn't hide from it any longer. I had to openly deal with it. I went into the hospital, and I talked to the doctors myself so that I could get an understanding of my mother's disease. After the conversation with the doctor, I was much more informed of the situation and more educated about its cause and origin. As a result of mother's illness, I went to school to study psychology. I remember my first and true understanding of my mother's horror. My Psychology professor delivered this analogy to me, and this is what she said,

"Schizophrenia is different from most mental illnesses in this way. Consider that all other illnesses are like tearing a piece of paper into bits and pieces and throwing it down on the ground. Now take the pieces and glue/tape them back together. You can make the paper whole again. Now imagine taking a glass jar and going to the top of a building and dropping it. Come down from the building and gather the pieces. You will never recover every piece. That's how people are who have schizophrenia. They take medicine like every other person that has a mental disturbance, but they still exhibit some symptoms. They never fully recover."

I went home that day and explained that scenario to my husband. My husband never really knew that my mother had a mental illness. Every time he saw her, she was doing fine. She had a lot of moments when she didn't hear voices, and these were the most peaceful times of our lives, especially when she had apartments of her own. She periodically went to the hospital, but the stays got shorter. I'm not sure if the medical profession got better, or they just knew what she needed. They had experimented with her for so many years. They just had the right mixture waiting on her.

Chapter 9

In 1997, my grandfather died. He passed away on September 1, and Mother started with a relapse. Her boyfriend had gotten locked up for welfare fraud and had developed esophagus cancer. He too died in October, and Mother totally lost control. She stopped taking her medication, and she went on a rampage like no other. The rantings and chants were strong, and she lost all sense of self. She didn't know who she was or that she was in the world. My family and I went home for Christmas, and Mother had not taken her medication for two months, and when I entered into her apartment, she was in the bed fully dressed with her coat and boots on, and she was partially unconscious. She had a new boyfriend, but he was not familiar with her condition. He just let her lie in the bed because he didn't know what to do for her. He was on drugs, which sort of had him out of the loop.

Immediately, my husband and I started praying for her. "In the name of Jesus, we rebuke thee Satan. Come out of her. By the Lord Jesus's stripes you are healed." We could hear the voices moaning within her. It was rather strange to me. Because for the first time, I could hear the voices that my mother heard for years. It was like some sort of exorcism. I could feel the dark presence of evil escaping from the bowls of her womb. Maybe it's because I was much more spiritual. The voices sounded like demons making funny noises, and I could feel them escaping as we prayed. My husband and I were doing spiritual battle.

"Loose her, Satan, I command you. Let her go." These were the words of a frantic daughter who so desperately wanted to see her mother free. She, at that time, had been tormented for twenty-three years. It's definitely the demons in a person's mind that keeps them bound with voices. What else could it be? Things were becoming very clear to me about what I had been really dealing with all those years. The prayer had shaken the house upside down so much so that the boyfriend got scared and called my granny to find out if my husband was a preacher or something. Mother slowly gained consciousness. However, she was not herself. I got Mother up and helped her to bathe and put on clean clothes. I took her to my grandmother's house because my grandpa had not long passed away, and I wanted to see my granny. I kept Mother from returning to the hospital because it was the holidays, and I wanted her to be with the family. We entered the house, and my kids ran to hug their grandma, but she was not there.

"What's wrong with Grandma?"

"Yeah, what's wrong with her?"

Both of my kids noticed a change in her appearance and her demeanor. She didn't hug them like she always had. She just looked at them as if she was looking through them. "She looks funny," said my daughter.

My kids were wondering what was wrong with their grandmother. They had never seen her like that. That was the day that my kids gained the knowledge that their grandmother, the person who had baked them cakes and sent presents all their lives, had a deep dark secret that was well hid even from them—mental illness.

"Your grandma is sick," I went on to explain. "She has a mental condition that causes her to not understand things around her. She still loves y'all, and she is still Grandma. She just needs to see her doctor and get some medicine. Then she will be herself again." There I was, explaining to another generation the problems that those voices had caused. I felt as though I was back at the moment of explaining it to my little brother. I was at the moment of truth. It was time the kids knew. They really didn't understand, but they knew that something was terribly wrong. She was not the grandma that they knew. She was withdrawn and talking to those voices. She didn't recognize her own grandchildren. She was ranting and raving about her dead boyfriend and how nobody in the family liked him. Quite the opposite. It was he who had kept her sane the longest. It was he that had given us some peace in our lives, and for that, I will, we will, be eternally grateful. Her mind was confused.

We enjoyed the holidays and went home. My grandmother tells me that as soon as we left, Mother went on a rampage. She picked up a bowl of hot water from the sink and threw it on my grandmother and replied, "I'm going to drown your butt." She then ran into the refrigerator and knocked the door of the hinges leaving my grandmother no choice but to call the police and have her committed.

Chapter 10

After Mother had gone into the hospital, she went back three more times before I made the decision to relieve my then seventy-nine-year-old grandmother from the torture that she had endured and bring Mother to live with me. That was when my family saw a whole new side of her. They got to experience what I, my brothers, and our grandmother had experienced for thirty-three years.

When we went to my grandmother's house for our yearly summer visit, it was the normal visit that we scheduled every year. There was no intention on bringing Mother to live with us, and I had no idea that she was in the state of mind that she was in. Mother had not taken her medicine. She hadn't changed her clothes in several days nor had she eaten anything, and she was after my grandmother again. Her mind had left her. She did not know the days of the week. She couldn't tell me when she had eaten or taken her medicine last nor could she count her money.

"Momma, where is your medicine?" I asked.

"What medicine? I don't need any medicine. They need the medicine. They around here talking about somebody crazy. I'm not crazy. They the one who's crazy," she replied.

"They who, Momma?"

"Oh, now you don't know who they is, them, they whoever."

It was at that moment I knew I had to do something. What? I didn't know. My head was spinning, and my heart was pounding with hurt, confusion, denial, and that feeling of darkness was taking hold of me as if it were choking the very life from my body. Fear gripped me like a big-time wrestler, one that had the winning grip of death during the final round of the show. This situation had to be dealt with by me. No longer could I continue to be on this roller coaster at the horror park. Mother's life was at stake, my own sanity was at stake, and my family's peace was at stake.

I began looking around the house for the medicine which I found in the garbage. Granny told me that Mother hadn't eaten in two or three days. She was frail and agitated.

"Momma, I need you to eat for me."

"Eat what?" she said.

"I will buy you some chicken from Popeye's," I replied.

"Okay, I ain't eating nothing from that kitchen. That witch is trying to poison me. That food smells funny."

I knew she was talking about my grandmother. Every time she became delusional, it was always my grandmother who was out to get her. This time she referred to her as a witch. She had never called her a witch before; therefore, I knew that she was far gone. I went to get Mother some chicken, and she ate it. I convinced her to take a shower and change her clothes.

After everything had settled down, I knew I had to have a talk with my husband.

"Larry, I need to talk to you." We went into the dining room and sat at the table. "I really need to bring Mother home with us. She is too much for Granny to handle anymore, and there is no one else that could take care of her better than us. I need to take her. For how long, I don't know. I do know that she cannot live here anymore." Then I rested to hear his response.

"This is your mother, and whatever you need to do, I'm totally with you. Tell me what you need from me, and I'll do it."

At that moment, tears filled my eyes. They dropped so rapidly they could have filled a ten-gallon bucket in minutes. How could I be so blessed to have a husband that would take in my mentally ill mother without knowing the full scope and sequence or the implications that it would have on our lives. We brought her home with us and experienced lots of chaos, but eventually, she became stable. She moved back to Cincinnati under the care of my dear aunt.

Once back home, she had fewer, yet more intense episodes. When she had them, Grandmother was still the enemy. She often called me on the phone with the "voice talk," and I would begin to pray right on the spot, which seemed to help. My mother lived in her own apartment until recently in the same senior building that another sister who had mental illness lived as well. She was bipolar. When they both lived with my grandmother, she had hell on her hands. Grandmother and my aunt are now deceased.

Mother will be mentally ill for the rest of her life, and the questions I have asked have been answered. She can live normal if she takes her medication regularly, but she will, because of the chronically disturbing nature of her illness, always experience some symptoms. She resides in a nursing home facility because the illness has evolved, and she now has dementia. She is regularly going back and forth to the hospital with pneumonia and flu symptoms because she smokes. Her mind is somewhat sound due to the around-the-clock care she is now receiving. As in the past, she does not have the will to live and has signed do not resuscitate paperwork and has shared her unwillingness to be on life support.

The family curse has struck again in my own son. Only God and the person who is experiencing the demons in their mind knows what it is like.

About the Author

Tina Harmon holds a master's degree in education. She works for a local school district where she helps special needs students and students who are mentally challenged receive their education alongside their general education peers. She has been married for thirty-three years and has two children and six grandchildren.

www.ingramcontent.com/pod-product-compliance
Lightning Source LLC
Chambersburg PA
CBHW031241120626
46545CB00003B/1229